LAUNCH IT

300+ things I've learned as a Designer, Developer and Creative Director.

A handbook for digital creatives.

Shane Mielke

Copyright © 2017 Shane Mielke
http://www.shanemielke.com
All rights reserved

Table of Contents

Intro

I did not sit down with the intent of writing a book. None of this content was premeditated or written specifically for this book. It was summertime, and I was on vacation with my family in Santa Cruz, Ca. We had stopped at a small local bookstore to buy some books and magazines to read over the next few days. While paying, I noticed a stand next to the register that had several small impulse buy books for sale. One, in particular, caught my eye. It was titled **"101 things I learned in culinary school"**. Something about the simplicity of the book and it's title made me stop and think.

I realized that over the course of my life, I had given a lot of advice to people in several different formats. For years I had been responding to emails from people asking me for guidance on topics like my creative process, inspiration, how to get a job, handling clients and self-promotion. I had also been lucky to do quite a few interviews & conference presentations that covered many of these topics. I hadn't realized it until that moment, but I already had the assets necessary for a similar book about design.

As a Creative Director and High School Football Coach of 16 years, it is in my blood to help mentor, teach and guide others. I love the passing on of knowledge to those around me. So I went back through those old emails, interviews and presentations to grab any advice, tips or comments I could find. Anything I felt might be useful to someone in our industry. What follows are some of those bits of advice from a period of over 15 years.

Some of these might be things you've already learned. Maybe you've heard something similar before. Some of these might sound redundant but are worded differently. It's possible you've just forgotten something you've learned or lost your forward momentum and need a reminder.

Depending upon your skills or job you might read the word **"designer"** but you need to process the advice as **"developer"** for it to make sense or apply to you. Other tips might not apply to your current professional/personal situation but might be valid later in your career.

Please read each comment on its own. Separate from anything else said before it. Whatever your current situation, my hope is that something here helps you launch or re-launch your motivation, process, goals, or career in some way. If there are any subjects I don't cover or if you have any questions, please email me. I'd love to hear your thoughts on the book and any ways I could make it better.

Best of luck and have fun.

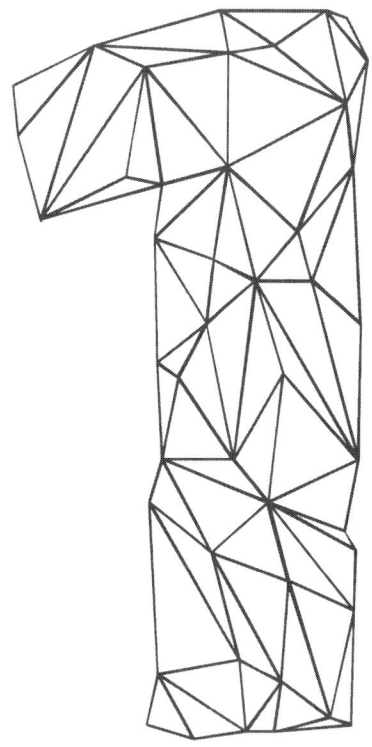

MOTIVATION & WORK ETHIC

Mental preparation for success

You are only as good as your last project.

Experience is earned.

Everyone wants to work on those once in a lifetime epic award-winning projects that everyone talks about. No one tells you that the road to those projects is paved by the mistakes and victories you achieve on all of the ordinary projects that came before it.

Fall in love with the grind.

You must be willing to put in extra time when you're the youngest or least experienced designer in the agency or on a project. There are no shortcuts to working on the cool projects. Take on as many different tasks as they are willing to give you. It doesn't matter how big, small, cool or dull those jobs are. That's how you get better, gain trust and more importantly, learn your limits.

.04

Opportunities for better projects start in "The Lab".

Design is a competitive field. Grow at a faster pace by experimenting outside of regular work hours. Play around with unconventional design styles, video, 3D or WebGL. Then share those experiments for everyone to see. Not only will this give you increased visibility but also perceived expertise within an area that can and will lead to projects utilizing those skills.

.05

Insecurity is normal.

We all think our work isn't as good as it could be and that every project we've done could be better. Don't let insecurity stop you from showcasing your work.

Even famous designers we look up to, have others they look to for inspiration.

Everyone has someone they look to and think, "I wish I were as good as them. I want to do the type of work they're doing". We're all humans with inspirations and insecurities.

Dedication, passion and commitment are equally as important as artistic talent.

Ultimately, an average designer with passion and dedication willing to put in the extra time and attention to a project can be every bit as good (or better) than an amazing designer who is lazy, unmotivated or uninspired.

You control your destiny.

Nothing is stopping you from being a great designer except for the excuses that you formulate in your head. When professional projects at work turn bad, create projects at home. Make things you have fun creating that develop the style of work people will recognize you for. Take a chance. Keep working hard and be passionate about getting better.

.09

Stay humble and always give respect and kindness to everyone around you. You never know when you might meet again or need their help.

.10

Work harder & longer than everyone else in the agency and you will eventually be rewarded with opportunities to work on bigger and better projects.

Be the best designer you can be at whatever style of work makes you happy.

Launches are often anticlimactic.

Hours, weeks and sometimes months of hard work go into projects. You should be happy and excited to see it all go live. But bad client decisions, short deadlines and other variables can quickly affect the final product giving you a nervous or sad feeling that taints your emotional memory of a project. All you can remember are all of the cool ideas left on the client's cutting room floor that didn't make it into the site. These are hard feelings to get over. But learn to love and embrace the projects you've worked on for being that best that you could give within their constraints.

Love what you do and infuse your passion, life and personality into each project regardless of the outcome or how big or small a project may be.

Be prepared. Work hard. Love what you do. Finish every project.

Never be too proud to analyze yourself.

Take an honest look at your habits, experience and skills to determine what is truly holding you back from achieving your goals. Then be strong enough to take action on those observations to change the things that are not working.

Set up both long & short term career goals along with an action plan of how you will accomplish them.

Long-term goals are important things like getting a job at your favorite agency, awards, magazine/book features, salary increase or job promotion. Short-term goals are education, skill or stylistic improvements. Constantly evaluate goal progress to objectively see if you need to change your plan, process, attitude or work ethic to accomplish them.

Goals must be observable, clearly measurable and attainable otherwise they're just dreams.

Goal overload can be just as counterproductive as having no goals.

Nothing changes if nothing changes.

Success is uncommon. Therefore success is only experienced by uncommon people or efforts.

Doing the bare minimum always returns average results.

Doing this repeatedly in your designs becomes a bad habit which is hard to recover from. "Do whatever it takes" is an attitude, a lifestyle, belief system and a choice you must make every day. Put in extra efforts that others might not give to increase your odds of getting noticed and making an impact on an otherwise average project.

Actions speak louder than words. Don't talk about producing great work. Do great work. Or at least be on the pathway towards learning how to produce great work.

Promote your work. Otherwise, no one will ever know you were a part of the project.

Becoming one of the best designers in the world is the most effective way to stand out from everyone else.

But it won't happen overnight. You must be unique and have the best skills, style and portfolio which all come by embracing the grind in your free time when no one else is watching or working.

Average is the opposite of great. Ordinary work will rarely achieve great attention.

Everyone wants to be a game day hero but nobody wants to practice.

You can't please everyone working on the project.

Trying to do so is usually a direct pathway to mediocre creative and failure to meet expectations. The only opinions that matter are those of the client and the user.

Do great work or expect to be overlooked for others that do.

EVERY project has the potential to change your career for better or worse.

Treat every project as an opportunity to do something special instead of only putting your best into what you feel are the important projects or big name clients. You never know which project will define your future (good or bad) so put your best into each one.

Successful personal projects are often the results of anarchy against bad daytime jobs, projects & clients. Turn bad work situations into positive personal ones.

Talent and skill are important, but you can't reach your full creative potential as a designer without drive & ambition.

.32

You can always handle more than you think.

Stretch the limits of your current design abilities by taking on more work and responsibility than your comfort zone allows. Much like building muscle requires adding extra weight and repetitions while working out. So does your growth as a designer with all of your skills.

.33

Praise is fleeting. Accept praise for your work, but ignore it because it will stunt your drive and personal growth.

Accept criticism but don't absorb it if it's not valid to the wider vision of a situation that only you truly know.

Make more time.

Take a week and do the following: Eat lunch at your desk instead of going out. Stay off social media like Twitter & Facebook. Only open & respond to emails 3x a day. Turn off the TV and stay away from YouTube. Avoid mobile, or console games. All of these things bleed small amounts of time every day. When added together those tiny bits form big chunks of time which could be used for any number of things both professional or personal.

Fear is the mind killer.

Your insecurities, fears and doubts are limiting your potential and ultimately your career. You must **believe** you can create award winning work, be featured in magazines or work at the best agencies for those goals to be real possibilities.

If one of your goals isn't to produce award winning work, you most likely won't produce any.

There is no perfect moment or client. Stop waiting for one. Take action on your thoughts without waiting for the perfect time.

If someone in the industry is better than you, it's likely they've worked harder or longer than you to get there.

Raw talent is important but work ethic and experience over time are more essential in creating a successful design career.

Keep Dreaming. Stay Hungry.

When your design dreams of winning an award or being featured in a magazine become your reality, they are no longer your dreams. Do not settle. Avoid resting upon your past. Keep cultivating new goals and moving forward with new passions.

.42

Good designers don't need to hear from others that they're good.

Experience and knowledge breed confidence. That confidence sheds the desire to seek acceptance and confirmation from others that you know what you're doing.

.43

Experience criticism and grow from it.

If you avoid criticism by never putting yourself out there with a portfolio, you'll never feel pressured to develop your skills to their full potential. You need that fear of being judged and having your work critiqued to push you to grow higher.

.44

You only have a few real opportunities in your career to do something special.

Your windows are small. Seize every opportunity and pretend every project is your last chance to prove what you can do.

Doubt in yourself will lead to doubt in your work. This leads to an inability to sell your ideas and doubt by the client that your designs are what they are looking for.

Have passion for every project.

You can always tell when a design, movie, song or piece of art was created by someone who was passionately having fun in the creation process. When others see and feel that excitement mixed with your blood, sweat and tears the project will shine even brighter. **Don't go through the motions.**

Criticism is fuel.

Some mentors, friends, coworkers or employers will try and motivate you by saying you "can't do" something. Make sure to recognize this situation for what it is. Process such comments as **motivation** rather than getting caught up in petty, defensive thoughts. Drama & negativity will not make you any better, but if used properly, patronizing words can push you through boundaries you might not have knocked down alone.

The greatest motivation for being good at what you do isn't just more money or an important sounding title. It's the potential for increased freedom, choices & control over your life and the direction of your career.

When you put positive energy and extra work into a project, it will always come back and benefit you in some way. Occasionally in ways, you might not immediately comprehend and sometimes long after the work is done.

We all have excuses for why we haven't achieved a goal or dream.

But for the things that truly matter if you want them bad enough you will have to push aside the things that are getting in your way. Do what you have to do to get where you want to be. Otherwise, someone else will.

Leading is lonely but exciting. Following is crowded and boring.

Goals need to be openly talked about, fantasized over and reached for repeatedly to eventually become true.

Confidence is one of the most important skills necessary to being a creative lead on any project.

You must enter the gauntlet believing that your ideas, style and execution can and will win any project you touch. Then exude that presence to the client inspiring them to believe in your ideas.

Be the best at what you do and set your own rules.

If you are the best person in the room at what you do, then you can set your own rules. As your job title goes up, so does the money you make. But more importantly, so does the control you have over your work when it gets done, how it gets done and what gets presented to clients. If you're just the lowly "designer" on the project, you should expect to be ordered around by project managers, clients, bosses and everyone else above you. The higher up you are, the more control you can fight for and the more protective you can be about how you give up your time. But you have to be able to back it up. If you're missing deadlines or bombing projects you've got bigger problems to worry about than keeping your life in balance.

Money and success should never consume or change you. Both can potentially strip away your drive for creativity and alter the person that brought you those accomplishments in the first place.

Unsolicited sincere compliments mean more.

Never fish for compliments on your work. Most people will only ever say what you want to hear which might not be what you actually need.

Consistently producing influential work requires an attitude that says "I will not compromise my standards."

It takes constant vigilance and effort because producing uninspired work is a downward spiral towards mediocrity. It is a disease acquired thru repetition and a habit that should be avoided because the result is that no one will care about you or your work.

Do something seven days in a row to create a habit.

Identify something you'd like to learn or work on. Challenge yourself to set aside time for it seven days in a row. If it's important, you will find a way to make it happen. This will build momentum and hopefully become something you see through to completion.

Believe in yourself and your personal style. Trust in your creativity and the purpose of your passion.

Keep moving, living, growing and expanding your horizons.

You can be on the pathway you dreamed of, but when you stop in the middle of that journey, you might as well be lost or have never started. You may work at one of the best agencies in the world but if you're going through the motions producing average work you're not taking advantage of that opportunity.

Nothing important comes without a lot of effort and maybe some pain.

If you want to reach a goal that is worthwhile, it's going to take time. It also takes an ability to get up off the ground when something bigger than you has put you there. If you're not ready, you have to make yourself ready. You must avoid being intimidated; you must have confidence in yourself.

Set new goals so that your best work is not behind you but yet to come.

Don't let a fear of change hinder the steps you need to take to achieve your dreams.

Few people know how or are willing to make the sacrifices it takes to be a great designer. You must put in the time and develop the skill to get the rewards.

When clients make bad design decisions, you must have the ability to accept a temporary defeat.

To understand that it's temporary without quitting. To recognize maybe you've lost the battle but the war isn't over and that you must keep fighting for your designs.

In design critiques, you will benefit more from being told what you NEED to hear not what you WANT to hear.

Surround yourself with the best or the hungriest creative people you can find.

You are the average of your 5-7 closest friends. Choose the ones who will lift you up and grow, not pull you down like anchors.

Live wherever makes you and your family happy.

Don't feel pressured to work in major cities like San Francisco, New York, Los Angeles or even the United States to work on the best projects. The primary requirement is to be talented and unique. I have friends known around the world, who have been featured in books & magazines and have won countless awards working on high profile projects. These individuals live in places like Fresno, California; Peoria, Arizona; Helena, Montana; and Bay of Islands, New Zealand. If you're good, you control your destiny and you can live, work and thrive from wherever you want.

What's your dream and what's your plan? You need to have both.

Wake up every day excited to create beautiful work and control your creative destiny. Don't lose a single day standing still.

Go THROUGH challenges not around them.

The efforts and struggles of fighting through boring or damaged projects are what prepares you for success on the important projects.

Realizing you're not where you want to, needs to be motivating not paralyzing.

What are you willing to give up in order to achieve something you want to accomplish?

We are mentally, physically, emotionally and creatively all like sharks. The minute we stop swimming we die.

GROWTH & MASTERY

Education, process & skill acquisition

There are ALWAYS more assets. Good creatives find ways to create their own assets even when there are none from the client.

Inspiration can happen anywhere.

When searching for those big creative ideas, try and get away from the computer to just zone out while doing something athletic in order to free your mind of any limitations. Physical activities help push aside all of the internal and external noise that constantly bombards us all and hinders our creativity.

Focus your efforts.

Execute the majority of your style and page designs at one time in a design sprint. Revisiting design elements even a week or two later can lead to disjointed mismatching elements because your personal style and inspirations subtly change over time.

Keep moving forward.

When you get stuck in the design process, switch to other responsibilities such as cutting out assets, searching stock photography or organizational tasks. This helps you stay productive, prevents you from staring at a blank canvas and will ultimately free your mind to come up with ideas.

Empty your mind.

The time spent doing mundane tasks like organizing Photoshop layers and project assets are perfect for leaving your mind completely blank. This opens your mind for those cool concepts which end up defining a project. Who hasn't had a brilliant idea when preoccupied with something boring like driving to work? You also look more professional when you pass off assets to the client or another team member.

Don't design in the browser on long-term projects.

Organize all visual assets of the project in Photoshop before any animation or development begins rather than designing as you develop. This ensures that theme and visual representation are consistent throughout the design, rather than a mixture of things you might have been feeling over the longer time period it takes to develop the site.

Add layers of love.

Once a project lives, breathes, animates and functions as the client expects it to, take a step back from the project and revisit key areas adding a few "layers of love" to make the project exceed client expectations. This is accomplished by going over the project in successive waves adding fun, unique animations, details and further functionality until your deadline is reached.

Repetition fine tunes personal style and breeds confidence.

With every completed project you get better, faster and your experience allows you to begin seeing the design solutions in your head before you even start. Thus eliminating the time spent staring at the screen or surfing for inspiration wondering what you're going to do. This allows you more time to work on the details that will truly separate a boring project from an exceptional project.

Create a Visual Vocabulary.

Set up standards and rules for consistency of every visual piece of a project. Colors, fonts, button sizes, line spacing, margins, etc. all establish the visual vocabulary or style guide of a site. Once established, don't deviate from that vocabulary for any reason. Together these pieces play a big part in how cohesive the design is and how intuitive the site is to use. Consistent details matter.

Old School is just as important as New School.

Every technique/solution both old and new has a place in the bag of tricks we use to design & develop projects. We shouldn't get too caught up in using just the latest and greatest trends when delivering solutions for our clients because they aren't always the best option. The key is looking at each project individually and evaluating all of the goals and limitations like budget, timing, costs associated with various execution scenarios and skill sets of the people involved in the project. Use the solution that gets the job done within the limitations of the moment.

New or old techniques are only as effective as the experienced hands that implement them.

Distractions kill productivity.

Wasted time is like eating junk food. Eating a "Twinkie" is empty calories in your diet. One "Twinkie" from time to time won't affect you. But if you eat enough of them, you're going to gain weight and get slow. An hour lost with an empty activity at work must be taken later from your free time. Are those "Twinkies" worth it? Feed yourself with the right fuel like a professional athlete would. Unplug from social outlets like Email, IM, Youtube, Facebook, Twitter and other extraneous influences when you need to focus on getting something done. Turn off everything for 3-4 hours at a time and see how much work you get done. We live in a world where we feel obligated to respond to an email, IM or phone call the second you receive it. You have to break yourself of such junk food habits by prioritizing your deadlines and tasks above others.

Keep track of those random moments of inspiration, or else the ideas will be forgotten amongst all of the noise in our lives.

Technology is the icing on the cake.

Just like a good photograph can stir emotions, a kickass design stands on its own without needing animations or any technology to bring it to life.

Specializing allows you to focus on being the best at one thing.

Over the years your experience will exponentially pay off if you hold yourself to a high standard. If you are a designer, a possible downside is that you will always depend on others to help bring your projects to life. Which can be frustrating if where you work has not invested in the right caliber of people who can develop to the level you are trying to achieve.

Using UI kits and templates can help save time. But the more you use them, the more you depend on them and the less your work will stand out as unique.

You don't need Feedback. The most liberating moment for any designer is when you stop soliciting ideas and feedback from others and start gathering them from your heart, soul and intuition.

Protect your time.

Clients, bosses and project managers will always try to get more from you out of less time. Deadlines are important but always fight to preserve your time otherwise you'll sacrifice creativity.

Skills are developed and earned by doing tasks over and over.

No different than learning an athletic skill, learning to play a musical instrument or mastering a video game.

Your target audience is not the overzealous super-fan client or the design community. It is the skeptical indecisive user or first-time visitor whose trust and attention you need to gain.

First round designs should focus on general style, UX and significant problem-solving objectives rather than the tiny details.

Don't spend extensive amounts of time crafting the "perfect button" if your overall style, layout and user flow are not fine tuned. The more you sweat the small details, the more you'll fall behind in addressing the bigger issues which ultimately are what make a project successful.

Cultivate your personal style, technical skills, processes and problem-solving techniques so that your creativity can take over when inspiration strikes.

The biggest waste of time & money in any project is the inability to make decisions. Lead yourself, your team and your clients.

Fight for more design time.

While it's necessary to have a deliverable timeline for any work, sometimes it's impossible to speculate on the amount of time it will take to formulate the best creative solution. When asked for how long it might take you to design something always pad your time.

Perfect your workflow on projects that have extremely tight deadlines.

I call these projects "Boot Camps" because you survive by honing the processes and techniques you already know within a shorter time frame than normally comfortable. While stressful, the benefits of surviving boot camp projects are that you are faster and more confident in your core skills for the cooler projects down the road. An additional benefit is that it takes you less time to do more which maximizes your profit potential on later projects with fixed budgets.

You don't have to specialize to be a successful creative.

The challenge of learning and using multiple skills like design, front-end development, photography and animation all together is fun, exciting and empowering. While you'll never be "the best" in any single discipline, you won't ever need to rely on others to bring your ideas to life.

Every project has a personality, and it is up to you to create it.

The right personality or mood can help people remember a site, buy a product or trust a company. How we establish that personality is up to us. It is the result of things like layout, colors, fonts, photography, 3D, video, music, animations or interactions. All of these combine to create each user's emotional interpretation of a site. The more a person feels the specific emotions we want them to the more they will remember the project.

Do not focus on the "Design Community" liking the content, style or layout of a project. The only group that matters is the target audience and if they can actually use the site.

Never confuse tools with strategies.

WebGL, Canvas, Flash, Jquery, CSS3 and HTML5 are just tools used to execute the unique creative strategies and ideas that come from our minds to help fuel the success of a site.

A good idea with bad design rarely achieves the attention it deserves.

Consequently, good design can make any idea look interesting but can't salvage a bad idea from failure. Success depends on both being good.

All of the tiny little compromises over the life of a project add up to corrupt and deteriorate even the strongest designs.

The creative process is similar to the action of completing a maze. Sometimes you need to explore a pathway to learn that it isn't the right one so that you can backtrack and select the correct direction.

It is better to deliver unique, impactful & emotional creative rather than boring, safe concepts that anyone could do.

Once your work is associated with being boring or safe it's difficult to regain trust or interest that you can do better. Your clients will eventually move on to someone else who can actually elevate their brand like you should have.

Minimal "safe" designs usually lead to forgetful sites. "Hey, who designed that very minimal site with big typography we were looking at a week ago?"

"I don't remember. Which one?"

On personal projects always set a deadline and stick to it like you would a client project. If you don't have a deadline, you will rarely finish the project.

Avoid creative decisions motivated by budget or money.

Money clouds judgment and dilutes the creative process by ruling out options that might push the envelope.

You can have read every tutorial on the internet, but that won't make you a better designer until you've used that knowledge in a project.

If a bad client request like "make the logo bigger" threatens to "ruin" your work, then the design probably wasn't that good to begin with.

Being a one trick pony with only one design style or skill only works if you're the best person using that style and it's the hot trend at the moment.

Know more. Do more. Earn More. Have more fun.

A designer who can execute or influence the UX, UI, animation, photography, 3d and development of a project is a management level Art Director or Creative Director. They can control their professional destiny, the creative vision of their work and earn as much money as they want. Individuals who can only do singular things will eventually reach a glass ceiling of respect, knowledge and participation on their projects. They will also potentially grow frustrated as various aspects of a project are dictated by others.

To be considered for unique projects, showcase your creative diversity.

Anyone can learn basic UX, a few standard layouts and a generic design style for a specific medium. Unfortunately the variables of each project fluctuate and so do the mediums, styles, layouts and solutions necessary for success. Until you've proven you can design for that diversity, your project choices will likely be limited to past accomplishments. You won't work on an interactive WebGL experience for a movie if you've only proven you can design a children's mobile app.

Don't use Technology as an excuse.

Current technology limitations should never be an excuse for not dreaming up new and unique creative ideas, solutions, experiences or designs. There are always possibilities within every technology and we have more options now than ever before.

There is a difference between working effectively vs. efficiently.

Being **effective** means setting and achieving goals. Being **efficient** means you're achieving maximum productivity with minimum wasted effort or expense. Unfortunately you can be highly effective but be throwing 80 hours a week at a project. Or be highly efficient and doing average work because you're not putting enough time in. There needs to be a balance where you are crushing goals & deadlines but aren't killing yourself or not living life because you're working so much.

Efficiency is just as important as hard work.

The more efficient you are, the more projects you can open yourself up to over the course of the year. That translates to more opportunities to do great work that fills up your portfolio to hopefully gain you recognition, money and creative freedom. You never want to look back on a year of working on just one or two projects or nothing that you're proud of.

Even great ideas can yield bad results if the design execution is poor.

Not every project will make it into your portfolio.

But every project is an opportunity to improve on something. Even a boring project where you are doing production work is a chance to fine-tune your technical skills, speed, efficiency and process which will benefit you later on the special projects.

The target audience changes with each project and client and so should your style & solutions.

Sometimes the target audience is a focused group of individuals and it is easy to create designs catering to that group. Other times the audience is so large and diverse that there is no pleasing all of the users. In cases where the audience is too diverse or undefined, it pays to listen to the guidance and advice of the client to make sure you are pleasing and reaching the people that they perceive as the most important.

It's impossible to account for every single user's preferences.

Every individual in the world has a different take on a favorite color, font, design style, font size, music genre, etc... Combine all of these opinions together and the combinations are endless. Designing a site for every possible user group isn't possible without losing a lot of the soul and personality of a site. Don't be afraid to take chances or focus just on pleasing the largest percentage of the target audience.

There is always a deadline, hurdle or client limitation on each project.

We must do our best with the cards were given. Some projects turn out great. Some turn out like complete and utter crap. No project ever feels finished.

Experience can be the enemy of creativity.

Don't let your knowledge of what you know has worked or failed in the past limit you from coming up with a potential new idea in the future.

Design isn't just about creating a pretty image. It is a strategic exercise in finding the best combination of BOTH organizational problem solving and artistic style.

A true designer does both UX and UI design.

These two skills might unfortunately be divided where you work. But it all comes down to how much control you'd like to have in the creative process and how high you'd like to rise in the industry. The more tools, skills and knowledge you have, the more you can creatively contribute to or direct various aspects of a project. Do both UX and UI and you'll have more respect, earn more money and make a bigger difference on projects.

When asking for objective critiques of your work, try and focus the questions into comments on specific details.

Vague questions such as "So what do you think?" will often result in vague answers both positive and negative based on the other person's style that does not address the feedback you truly need. A better question is "What can I do to make this specific area better?".

Use whichever operating system, hardware or software works for you and your workflow.

I was once told, "Only creative people use MACS." I have always preferred using a PC. Using a MAC or PC indicates nothing about your potential or skill as a designer or developer. Neither platform is more/less creative than the other. If a certain piece of hardware or software works for you and you know how to use it, then it is the right one for you. Even if someone else claims their tool is better.

Just because trends exist among designers doesn't mean that people outside the design community (the real users) actually like them.

Make client work personal.

As long as you are doing predominantly "Client" work, you'll find yourself looking at other people's experimental personal projects with a bit of envy. If you can't do those types of projects for yourself, try to apply your ideas to viable work projects. Don't be afraid to suggest progressive enhancements or ideas you're inspired by that could actually improve the quality of a client project. What's the worst thing that could happen? The client says no. But at least you tried and possibly learned some new software or techniques that might make it into your next personal or work project.

The freedom to make your own decisions without needing the consent of a committee is one of the most powerful assets you can have on a project. Fight for that freedom to control your own creative destiny.

Having more than one role on a project allows you more control of the overall creative execution of a site and keeps your job from becoming boring and repetitive.

(moreTime != betterWork)

More time does not equal better work. Long projects with a surplus of time, meetings and group decisions can also end horribly. Some of the worst projects I have experienced were 6+ months while some of the best projects were two-week sprints.

Be open to all solutions when you are in the creative brainstorm phase of a project. Don't eliminate an option because you have too much or too little experience with a technology. Experience can work against you making your solutions predictable and boring.

Successful UI animations require a strong sense of rhythm.

Animation is not about what plug-ins, software or technology you're using. It's about timing, tempo and how you layer the movement of individual assets together in a way that harmoniously tells a visual story. This only comes with practice and experience.

Always finalize the functionality of a site before adding animations, interactions or transitions. A site can launch without all of the bells and whistles and still be a success.

College degrees are not necessary for success as a designer in this industry.

I have a college degree in Rhetoric and Communications. The student in me wishes that I had a degree or formal education in art or design. But I also feel that not knowing some things have helped me be more open to self-growth, experimentation and cultivating a diverse skill set. Half of my friends have a design education and the other half are self-taught like myself. Some people need the structure and guidance of a formal education system. Others are do-it-yourself types who need to move at their own speed and figure things out through trial and error. Neither way is perfect. Ultimately, success and beautiful work depends on the individual and how they grow, learn and create the best. How you gained your knowledge is not important. All that matters are your results and if your work is good or not.

Attend conferences with goals and a purpose.

Each conference has something to offer. But just like planning out the places to see on a vacation you have to organize your time to maximize your money and optimize the experience. In addition, meeting up with online acquaintances, prospective clients and speakers can all lead to future projects or jobs which easily cover the cost of admission.

Avoid conference sessions on topics you're already an expert at. You'll just reaffirm knowledge you already have. It's far better to attend topics on things you don't understand or that are outside of your comfort zone.

Even art schools produce bad designers.

Can a degree from an art school be a good thing? YES! Is one necessary? NO! What's truly important, is how hard you're willing to work in or out of school to learn the skills you need to survive.

You must be an expert at something to stand out.

Design, Photoshop, Motion, WebGL, Front-end development, Javascript, HTML/CSS are all singular skills to start with. Pick one thing to learn and know it like the back of your hand. Once you've achieved mastery with it focus on expanding that knowledge to as many things that work with, supports or relates to that skill. Grow outwards from that central point of interest. If you start by learning random skills that do not relate to one another, it will be harder to make them all work together.

Take on projects where you are forced to learn new skills that will benefit you later. Even if it's at the sacrifice of time, money and a few gray hairs.

Master one skill at a time.

The more you attempt to master several skills at once the greater the chance you'll end up being average at all of them. Spread out your learning by picking one skill and focus on it for a year or two. This could be any creative discipline like interactive design, print, HTML, Flash, illustration or Motion graphics or a specific type of design within any of these (Posters, Wallpapers, Websites, etc.). Complete focus and dedication to one program or skill for a year or more will leave you with experience, understanding and muscle memory of a discipline that will stay with you forever rather than just being average at several things.

Learning how to design is similar to learning how to play a musical instrument like a guitar.

You can take music lessons but most people further guitar skills by learning how to play their favorite songs and then practicing them over and over in their free time. As you learn more songs, you start to cultivate the style of music you like and eventually start making your own unique music.

Be a specialist with a unique skill or knowledge of a tool.

At an early job, I became known as one of the only people in the company who knew Adobe Flash. This paid huge dividends because instead of just being one of the designers on the team who had no voice in meetings, I suddenly was a valued opinion in the group. I could help set expectations, timing and creative visions for projects involving Flash. Anytime you can control your destiny and have a leading voice on a project you can also control what is expected of you and when it's due. Today's modern equivalents to Flash would be anything to do with WebGL, Canvas or tools like Cinema 4D.

Skills come from hours of experimenting with your ideas, observing trends, re-creating styles that might influence you and learning from all of the successes and mistakes you experience on projects.

Experience is earned thru repetition and hard work on REAL PROJECTS. Not from reading a tutorial.

Self perception is reality.

I wasn't always a designer. I started as a front-end developer who aspired to be a designer. I wanted to have the power to change the things about a design I didn't feel were right. Although I always considered myself creative, I continually felt inferior to others who went to Art School or college for design. In my mind, they knew what was right or wrong according to the principles of art and design while I just had untrained opinions. It took a lot of work and practice but I grew my design skills over several years. But even then I wasn't confident. It wasn't until I verbally started calling myself a designer out loud that I was able to start relaxing and shed my insecurities when I worked. Once I stopped listening to those internal doubts in my head my career as a designer took off.

No one will hire you for your hidden skills.

Don't hide the things you're experimenting with because you don't think they're good enough. If it's not visible in your portfolio or talked about by others, no one knows about it. It's the skills and knowledge you showcase that will gain you notoriety, respect and possibly more work.

Everything you need to learn to change your career is accessible for free on the internet. The answer to every question you might have, can be found by a simple google search. What are you waiting for?

Knowing the pathway to mastery that other designers have followed to achieve their success is valuable. But you really just need to know what is possible.

Then go and accomplish the same things your way but within your style, skills, strengths and weaknesses. Because there are many pathways available to achieve the same results. What might have worked for someone else might not work for you or even be an option available. Just because they had to work 80 hours a week working at a huge agency in San Francisco doing product design, doesn't mean that is the formula you need to follow. I created a name for myself working at a small agency near where I grew up in Orange County, California far away from the large cities where the big agencies exist.

Foosball is the Enemy.

At an early job when work stopped coming in, a lot of people spent time playing Foosball to pass the empty time in the day. I recognized early on that it was a waste of time playing a game that wouldn't benefit me in any professional way. Instead of playing or bonding with my co-workers, I spent my time learning Flash, CSS, animation and worked hard to become a better designer. Which eventually paid dividends and launched my career. Foosball is just a metaphor for anything in your day that might distract you or take your time. Long lunches, useless meetings, video games, Facebook and mindless surfing, are all things that when done excessively, affect how productive you can be and how good you are at your job.

The details matter.

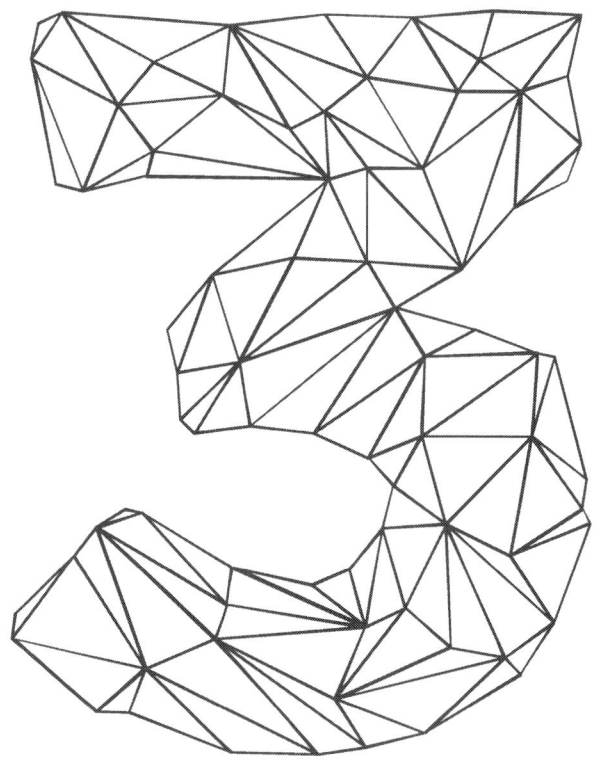

BE UNIQUE & STAND OUT

Individual style & self-promotion

Be Different.

It's ok not to see things the way others do. Your ideas, vision & style should be unique to you as a person and the things that inspire you. They shouldn't come from what someone else thinks you should do. Being different means that you have the potential to approach & create designs unique to you that will inspire others.

Your personal style is the only thing you truly have control over. Push your style without needing, wanting or waiting for the approval of others. Especially in personal projects.

Be observant of those who have been there before you.

There are many talented creatives who inspire us across different mediums and genres. Observe what they do and how they do it. Learn their techniques without directly copying their artistic style. Apply those techniques to your projects infusing them with your unique mixture of passion, experience and creative expression to form a new creative perspective.

There is only one you.

Don't try and do things exactly like someone else's work. Be aware of what makes you unique. It's your greatest gift and what will help define and separate you from others.

All critiques are welcome, but not all critiques are valid. Learn who you should and shouldn't listen to.

How can you stand out if your work looks like everyone else's?

Minimalism without personal style is just boring design.

The first step in developing a style that everyone recognizes you for is to stop ripping off the current trends that everyone else is doing.

Know your Style.

Tight deadlines are often the wrong situations to experiment with styles and skills that aren't already in your bag of tricks. When designing on a tight deadline "be yourself" by leaning upon your current skills, strengths, interests and personal style. Decisions can be made a lot faster if you have a well developed personal design style, codebase, process or even just a style guide for a particular project. One of the things that waste the most time on any given project is taking too long to make intelligent decisions. Sometimes that "looking for inspiration" stage can drag you down. If you have a strong personal style, you will enter projects already knowing the pathway you're going to walk down which can save you time. Doing so doesn't mean you're not creative or open to other options. It just means that you're able to optimize your time by not wasting it trying to figure out where to start.

.163

Observe, Listen & Learn.

Fight to stay open to new ideas, techniques and creative paradigms that will help your work grow in the future.

.164

When you start telling yourself "it's been done before" you've closed your mind to the possibilities.

Change your paradigm to be "it's been done before, but I'm going to do it better."

.165

Don't spread yourself so thin by obsessing about learning other people's styles and techniques to the point that you never really establish your own.

The only way to stay ahead of design trends is to create them.

Identifying, establishing and honing personal styles or techniques through repetition is what will separate you from the crowd who is just copying popular trends. Create your path and be the best at your style and others will notice you for it.

Our ideas aren't completely ours, and there is no such thing as an original idea.

We're all influenced by someone or something else, but we do have control over our individual styles which should never directly copy someone else.

It's okay to have one style as long as you don't mind working on the same type of projects over and over and over...

In a sea of creatives all influenced by the same trends, it takes a lot of effort to be unique and truly commit to a personal style that separates you from everyone else.

Once you're confident with your work, you will stop worrying about what other people think of it.

Such confidence becomes an unstoppable force in your ability to make faster and more effective decisions when you design.

Not being known in the design community is actually an opportunity to act without the pressure that comes from the expectations of others.

A reputation established by past accomplishments or styles can have a stifling influence on coming up with fresh ideas.

You will get more projects if people recognize your work for being consistently great rather than consistently the same style.

But if you are focused on one style it is better to be recognized for kicking ass with that style than not being recognized at all.

It's easy to hate on other people's work if you're not happy with your own style or situation.

The happier you are with your work, the more you'll appreciate and applaud rather than hate on what other's are doing, thinking or saying.

Develop a cohesive animation style for each project.

Pick an easing equation and stick with it throughout the site. Make sure that all objects of similar type (for example buttons) always animate with the same duration. Strive to make everything work in unison and animate to the same beat.

You don't need a "portfolio" to survive and get a job. But who doesn't want more $$$ and creative control of their destiny & work choices? Make the time.

Self-promote yourself even if it's not comfortable.

The biggest promotional tool a designer can have is a personal URL. It is vital to have a unique site that showcases your talent, skill, personality and creative vision outside the standardized portfolio templates that people use. It's important to promote your site then by being active in communities like Behance & Dribbble, submitting sites for showcases & awards like FWA & Awwwards, networking on Twitter or LinkedIn and submitting recent work to magazines.

Don't rely upon your day job to be your only creative outlet or sole source of work for a portfolio.

Sometimes it's necessary to fabricate your own work, website or personal art to gain a name and get a foot up into a better job. You need to sit down and brainstorm and create the best looking portfolio that you can make, even if that portfolio might not have much of your professional work in it.

The focus, presentation and contents of your portfolio can and should change depending upon your current professional goals. A portfolio that needs to get you a new full-time job should look a lot different than one geared towards selling personal art or gaining more freelance work.

Portfolio designs generally follow two formulas.

Option 1: A simple content oriented grid design with basic styles and fonts which do not compete with the work found within. In this case, the quality of the work itself is what gets you noticed and the site is just the framework. This is what most designers commonly do if they have a solid body of past work.

Option 2: A highly stylized design which showcases a unique individual perspective that possibly overpowers or hides the work within. This option is more likely to get you recognition or awards based on the emotion or experience of the site itself. The road less traveled is harder to do because it means ignoring or breaking current trends. Both can be effective.

Choose the one that best fits your personality or needs.

When deciding on where to start designing your portfolio, take a look at the type/style of work you'd like to be doing and then do that work for yourself. This will place you in the exact niche you want to be in.

Don't Blend in. Stand Out.

It's easy to take the safe road executing the trends and styles everyone else is doing. Unfortunately, most people don't get recognized for staying in the shadows. Unless your work is better than everyone else in the community doing the same thing, blending in won't get you the recognition you want.

If potential clients or the community don't see you or your work, then you don't exist. Neither will any opportunities for new projects or jobs.

Even if you're an introvert, you have to get eyes on your work in whatever way works for your personality. Not having publicly visible work gives you fewer career options.

When brainstorming portfolio or personal project ideas, start with a new style or topic you're passionate about. Try not to feel pressured to start where you think others expect you should based upon past work.

If your strategy for gaining new projects and recognition depends on someone discovering your work but all you have is a temporary splash page with no portfolio, then your plan will probably fail.

It takes hard work to become visible in the community, and it's even more difficult to stay both visible and relevant over time.

Portfolio platforms like Behance are simple and effective ways to showcase your work online, but there are drawbacks.

If your work gets featured, there are tremendous opportunities for recognition in the community. Unfortunately, not everyone gets featured, and there are drawbacks that should be considered. A huge downside to these networks is that your work is hosted among peers and companies that you might be in competition with for work. Imagine sending a client a link to your work on a hosted portfolio platform, and instead of seeing just your projects they start clicking the people in your own network or the featured pages. Then they find someone better or cheaper than you to do their project. Unless your work is better than everyone else around you, don't rely on them as your only portfolio.

Portfolio platforms help make people lazy to the point of not pushing their own portfolio sites as the initial point of contact with the community.

For most of us, our client work doesn't showcase our real personalities. As templates, neither do these hosted sites. So we should all have individual portfolios that allow us to visually and verbally separate ourselves from everyone else and tell the whole story of who we are. As the popularity of these communities increase, many people have forgotten this and are getting lost in the crowd.

If you only show the same style of boring client work in your portfolio, that is all you will be known for.

That is the only style of work that studios or clients will approach you for. The only way to break that view of your work is experimenting with and posting the type of work you'd rather be doing. Sometimes this means transforming a portfolio into an experimental website that in fact shows no past work and is simply a fun creative outlet.

You might have to design your personal portfolio 10x to find the best one for you.

But each time you **START** and **FINISH** a design you learn something about yourself and the process. Don't start, get frustrated and stop... Can you do that with a client or work project? No. We always have to finish something to learn from it. Even our personal stuff.

Student portfolios that are too diverse with nothing focused in one area don't show a prospective employer that they should take a chance on you.

I get the question a lot from students about how they should populate their portfolios to get hired out of art school. Focus your portfolio. A portfolio geared towards getting a job should either reflect the style of work that you want to be doing or the companies you want to produce work for. If you're hunting for a job at a studio that produces websites, show as many websites in your portfolio as you can. If those studios have a particular style, try and feature that style if possible. Eliminate or hide vague school projects, your first 3d render, mediocre photography or anything that doesn't highlight your strengths and what you might be doing in the company. Showing broad work from art school or work from other disciplines can dilute your content, presentation and impair your goal of getting a job.

We all have unlimited creative freedom.

There is nothing stopping you from creating an amazing personal site, personal brand, motion graphics video, experimental art or anything that embraces some wild idea that you have. You don't need to wait for a client to fill your portfolio with stunning work and you don't need someone else's approval that your idea is a good one.

Archive all projects online when they are done.

Be prepared for any situation. Process and archive screenshots from all of your latest work and post them on your portfolio even if they aren't publicly visible. You never know when you will need to easily showcase specific examples of recent work to a prospective client. Sometimes the difference between you getting a project over someone else is how quickly you responded to email inquiries with examples of your work. The freedom to respond immediately is liberating and makes the process stress free.

We all have free time in between projects. Use that time wisely.

It's the perfect time to focus on yourself and your visibility. Release personal projects or experiments. Update your portfolio with new work. Reconnect with former coworkers and friends on social media to show them your latest. Assume no one knows what you've been up to and do the things it takes to keep yourself on everyone's radar. Being relevant and active in your self-promotion is often the difference between having a steady stream of projects and not having anything to work on for a month.

When connecting with industry leaders & professionals on social media, don't forget to be interesting and even more importantly, GOOD at what you do. If the person doesn't know you personally, the quality of your work and portfolio is often the difference between being accepted or ignored.

You can't rely upon social media to tell your whole story.

People are busy, information moves fast and depending on your Twitter style, your important "latest work" tweets might be lost amongst your conversations. Don't assume that people are stalking you and have seen every photo, post, Dribbble or tweet you've made. They have probably only seen 1/10th of everything you've posted. Keep links to the important projects, experiments, code samples and posts organized and permanently visible in a portfolio. Because no one is going to go back across your social media to find them.

Projects that didn't live up to expectations can be reborn in your portfolio.

Creating case studies or portfolio entries filled with the best parts of a project that were never seen can often showcase the work better than the live site. This can also give you a cathartic feeling, helping to adjust the negative emotions and memories you might have about the project.

An award-winning portfolio has the potential to change your career and life.

We all know it's near impossible to come up with something unique for ourselves. It's why so many designers just go through the motions posting work on generic template portfolio platforms. What is lost by this is the chance to stand out because those types of portfolios will **never** gain you personal awards or recognition for the site itself. Those who dare to take their expertise and apply that knowledge to their personal brand have the unique opportunity to open up doors for themselves in ways they never imagined. An industry recognized award for your personal site immediately impacts the amount of respect you receive in the community and at work. Individuals who were at the bottom of the agency are suddenly respected and even promoted. Your opinions are suddenly valued, even though you're still the same person you were when they didn't listen to you. You might also get better projects coming your way and possibly a raise as management is worried you might take a better job. In my case, I immediately achieved a job at my agency of choice as well as features and interviews in books and magazines that changed my career, life and financial trajectory for years afterward.

Winning an award isn't the real goal. The confidence, perception, reputation and street cred which result from that award are.

Make cool shit for the love of creativity, and the money will come as a result.

Many people focus on money as their professional priority. They find jobs with a pretty title which pays them what they need or want but at the sacrifice of quality creative opportunities. They're making good money but working on boring, unchallenging projects while dreaming of doing more exciting work. I've never focussed on money. My passion has always been to work on as many cutting edge projects as possible no matter what they paid. The visibility, notoriety and creative freedom gained from this focus have always led me to more money. You do not have to sacrifice fun & creativity for more money. You can have both because the two go hand in hand.

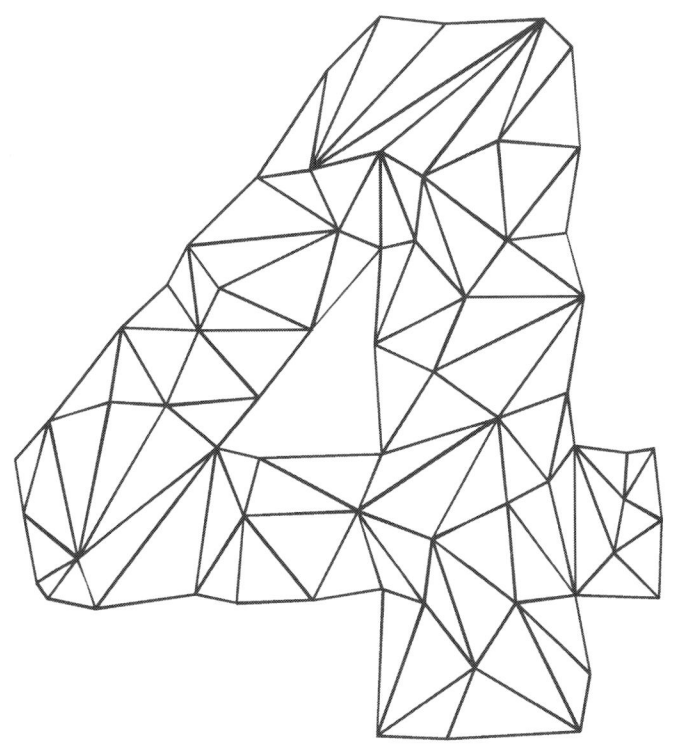

WORK
CLIENTS
FREELANCE

Navigating the professional world

Work for companies whose internal hierarchy work best for you, your career goals and your interests.

Larger companies or agencies often require specialization in a single role. This can be beneficial if your goal is to focus on the development of an individual skill like design. But beware as your sphere of influence will be limited to that one area. Smaller agencies value a more diverse skill set where you will have more responsibilities in a project potentially utilizing more of your interests and expertise.

Attitude is everything so always try and be aware of the type of energy you're expending.

No one wants to work with individuals harboring egos, disruptive personalities or personal baggage that negatively affects everyone around them no matter how good you are.

No matter how valuable you think you are, you're always replaceable. There will always be someone who wants your job, title, project or responsibilities and is willing to do it for less money.

Design by committee always results in watered-down solutions submerged by multiple personalities and conflicting feedback.

Don't insist upon greatness from others if you can't lead by example.

Agencies that stifle creativity by doing everything and anything the client wants without question, eventually lose that client to a company that will champion creativity, push back on their bad requests and give them what they really need.

Avoid working for companies who do not value investing time in solid creative, or you'll soon stop producing anything worthwhile.

The reputation of the company you work for influences your own reputation. Choose Wisely.

Everyone on the team is interesting and inspiring in some way.

Each person has a unique background with the potential to bring a new idea, inspiration, perspective or skill to the project. Treat everyone's ideas with respect. Even the annoying co-worker that you can't stand being around.

Embrace your relationships with your co-workers while you have them. Nothing ever stays the same. Everyone is on their own unique pathway. Friends will come and go from your professional career whether you like it or not.

Responsibility and trust are never automatically given. They are earned by continually proving your worth on both the good & bad projects you're involved on.

.211

The employer/employee connection is a symbiotic relationship where each party should need, want and benefit from the existence of the other.

When that is out of sync it's time to repair the relationship or move to a place that's working for you as much as you are working for them.

.212

Try not to work for unethical or dishonest people. You'll either become that yourself or everyone will assume you're guilty by association.

If you ever find yourself working for a company who doesn't respect you or isn't working towards your personal/professional goals, it's time to consider looking for one that does.

There is no shame in leaving an unhealthy working environment.

Too often we just take our paychecks, suffer through an endless stream of bad projects, or endure working situations that are really not in sync with our long-term goals. All because that's what good employees are supposed to do for the good of the team. **Not true.**

Take important discussions or presentations offline away from emails or chat and onto the phone or in person. To truly sell your ideas, perspective or yourself, people have to hear the passion in your voice or experience it in person.

Love what you do.

If you love what you do, you will never work a day in your life. But be careful not to let what you love rule your life. It's easy to overwork when you're having fun being creative to the point that you don't have a real life outside of work.

When leading a team, clearly vocalize what you're trying to accomplish and what you need your teammates to do so that all goals and tasks are out in the open. If you hold un-verbalized expectations of people they will always end up disappointing you in some way.

Avoid companies or clients that don't allow you to have a portfolio or post your work. Yes, you are getting paid, but you're limiting your future opportunities by being irrelevant.

Working for a large agency or brand can potentially create a lot of opportunities for experience and be a great name on your resume.

On the flip side, it also means more collaboration, decisions by committee and less control over your creative. All experiences are important but the knowledge you gain from projects with more personal control and ownership are a lot more valuable over time.

.220

Don't take career advice from someone that you wouldn't trade places with professionally.

.221

Office politics suck but sometimes you must be able to play the games and run with the wolves to move up the food chain.

Job frustration can be a powerful motivator if you use it to your advantage.

Rather than complaining about a bad situation, take your energies and focus them in a direction that solves the problem. Otherwise, switch gears and use that frustration as inspiration for a personal project or new portfolio. Life is too short to spend time unhappy. Never sit and wait until things get better if you don't have to.

Don't be that guy. There is nothing worse than working with a talented person who is difficult, moody or closed to exploring alternate solutions to problems.

When fighting for an idea at work, you have to know what stepping over the line costs and when to cross it. Being rebellious about the right things for the right reasons is not a bad thing.

Don't be lazy with your file organization.

There are truly no excuses for messy or disorganized source files. Always organize your assets as well as descriptively name your folders & layers. It doesn't matter if you're on a huge team or the only person on a project. The more organized your files are, the easier they are for you or others to work with if you have to revisit projects months later. It's a matter of respect and personal pride, and it only takes seconds during or after a project. Can you imagine if a developer had a function called "Copy of Layer 368" in their code? Would you employ a housekeeper that cleaned your house by hiding trash in drawers?

You don't need to switch jobs every couple of years to upgrade your salary and title.

As long as you're happy, challenged and executing solid work then there is nothing wrong with staying at the same company and rising up the ranks with hard work and a solid reputation for always delivering. As other people leave the company there is the potential for your role, salary and title to go up all without having to start over at another company in another city.

With every new job comes the stress of having to give 110% to prove yourself to a new group of people.

Constantly changing jobs might bring you a slightly higher salary or a better title but it can also make your life more difficult. With each change the pros, cons and responsibilities of your job also change. It can be even more stressful if your job is in a new city that you need to move for. Sometimes stress and change might not be worth a few thousand dollars extra a year. Evaluate your options and choose wisely.

Surround yourself with people who have the skills you want, the same goals you have or are the type of people you want to be.

Misery loves company, and that goes for the good-hearted successful people who are at the top of their game, and the negative people who sit at the bottom wondering why they never accomplish anything significant.

Project Managers exist to help manage clients, deadlines, communication and projects in general.

While their experience and opinions as users are valid for things like usability, project scope & content, don't let them micromanage or dilute the personality or design style of the site from the vision in your mind.

The most effective ways to get freelance projects are from past work, friends and prior client relationships.

Many talented designers struggle to get work simply because they do not have a network of relationships from these areas established. As your relationships grow so does your business as long as you hold yourself to a high standard producing solid work while also being trustworthy, dependable and finishing projects on time and on budget.

Always charge for your knowledge, experience and creativity.

Doctors, Lawyers and mechanics charge for their time and so should you. Just because most of us would be creative for free doesn't mean we should be.

Do good work, treat your clients with respect, meet their goals, finish projects on time and on budget and it's likely you'll get more work.

Deadline, budget and creative opportunity are all important factors to weigh before taking on a project or client.

Does the deadline work within the free time you have? Can you complete the job without killing yourself with all-nighters? Do you need the money specifically for something you've been saving for? Is the project paying what you're worth? If it's a freelance project on top of a full-time job is the money enough to merit using evenings and weekends away from friends & family? Finally is the project a unique opportunity to do something new? Or is it something boring that you already have several examples of? Will the project potentially make it into your portfolio and help you get more work in the future? Ask yourself all of these and then weigh out the answers to make a logical decision.

If you've established a reputation of doing solid work in the industry, have confidence knowing that you're good enough to get another full-time job if you want or need one. Don't be afraid to say goodbye to that job or boss you're unhappy with currently.

Deciding to go Freelance doesn't always happen as the result of a landslide of potential projects that suddenly come your way.

When everyone knows you're a full-time employee, many potential agencies and clients will not consider you a viable freelance asset. It's difficult to trust someone with a project knowing that the work will be completed in your free time on nights and weekends. If no one is knocking at your door, it's hard to make the leap of faith to go Freelance full-time. The scary reality is that you often have to make the jump and publicly announce that you've left your current employer before the work will start coming to you.

Weigh the pros and cons of large vs. small.

Securing large projects with big brands doesn't automatically bring happiness or mean cool projects. Bigger clients have more money, but it typically means more people are involved. That means more individuals who want to dictate the creative all the way down to the tiny silly changes that make you want to pull your hair out. I prefer smaller projects with greater creativity and control.

The perfect client has a manageable deadline, huge budget and a unique project for you to stretch your wings creatively.

Unfortunately, there is a sliding scale and projects rarely match up in all 3 of those categories. The biggest paying projects have the worst deadlines and low creativity. The most creative opportunities have the smallest budgets and take up the most time. Make decisions based upon what you want & need at the time but never be afraid to pass on something that doesn't feel right.

Clients or agencies ultimately hire you because they can see themselves, their products or their ideas in your style of work.

Showcase your work appropriately for the agencies you want to freelance for and type of work you want to be doing.

If you are not receiving emails liking or requesting your work, you unfortunately do not exist.

Accept the challenge to change the situation by any means that excites you. Try something new you've never done before. It won't happen overnight, but portfolio redesigns, new personal art, blog posts, case studies, demo reels and project updates are all great starting points for fighting your way back into visibility one step at a time.

Freelance or full-time, you are your own business and time is valuable.

As a freelancer, you might bid on a project based upon the time you think it will take you to complete the task. Then imagine that the project goes 2x longer than you anticipated. You just lost time potentially used on other projects which in turn costs you money impacting your profits. As a salaried full-time employee, you have a fixed yearly income that doesn't change. But if you're on several projects with long deadlines, that means fewer projects in a year that you can showcase in your portfolio. Reducing your visibility and how marketable you are in the future in getting a better job that pays more. In both situations, this is compounded if any of those projects end up being bad enough that you don't even claim them. Freelance or full-time, your time and what you do with it affect you in some way.

Under promise then over deliver.

Overpromising to a client only leads to disappointment should you not meet their expectations. Listen more and say as little as possible and then exceed expectations.

If you're a talented, organized, networked, self-motivated individual, you can make a lot of extra money by freelancing on top of a full-time job.

Especially if you don't have a family that needs your free time. Having a full-time job allows you to accept only the projects you have time for, are interested in or that have budgets that match your personal needs.

Respond to all emails and inquiries even if you are booked solid with work.

There is no commitment to having conversations about potential projects and start dates. It often takes days or weeks to go from contact to kickoff. This is often the time spent finishing your existing projects.

When a freelance project ends there can be sadness as you realize that you will no longer be interacting with the people you just collaborated with for the past few months.

It can be emotionally painful as you realize that even though you felt like it, you weren't really a part of their company's full-time team. Those friendships are real and the day to day interactions can still occur just without the purpose of a project behind them. Keep in touch because you never know when you might be needed again.

What you earn is limited to what you can or can't accomplish every day.

The more projects you can successfully manage over the course of the year, the greater your potential income. The most successful freelancers are able to juggle multiple projects at the same time while still meeting expectations and deadlines.

Clients do not need to know about your other projects as long as the work is getting done properly.

Can you successfully balance multiple projects at the same time without killing yourself or sacrificing quality? If so, just keep your head down, be quiet, do the work and cash the checks. Just don't be the person on the project who is obviously not pulling their weight. You won't get more work from that client.

You need to have personal experience with the maximum number of projects you can successfully manage at one time. Know your physical & mental limits. As a freelancer, this will help you know when to say yes or no to new projects. It will also help you calculate your maximum earning potential.

Schedules can be adjusted.

If you're booked but you really want to work on the project, don't be afraid to discuss your current workload and deadlines. Maybe your responsibilities can scale with your available time. If the client really wants to work with you, it will work out. If you were just "another designer" for the project, they will move on in the blink of an eye.

Get written confirmation at the beginning of a project whether or not you will be able to publicize the work.

Not only is it a legal matter, but a positive or negative response sets the tone for how emotionally invested you are in the project. If you go in knowing you can't tell anyone about the work you're less likely to hold the project on a pedestal.

Always consult with the agency you did the work through before publicizing a project.

They're the reason you worked on the project in the first place. Get their blessing on how you promote the project. You don't ever want to tweet or promote in ways that make you appear like competition to the agency. Not only can things get messy but it will likely mean no future work even if the project in question was successful.

Perfect clients are hard to find.

The ideal client knows their business, brand and project goals. They let you meet their goals by allowing you to infuse your personal vision & style into the project without micromanaging or tweaking all of the tiny and unexplainable artistic details that come from years of experience and intuition. They also want you to create award-winning work and have the assets to back it up. These are rare situations to come by so enjoy them when they happen.

Never force a client into a style that you want but they have reservations about.

It can and will come back and bite you. Meaning you have to re-do all of the work. There is a balance between maintaining your creative integrity by infusing a project with your ideas and style while also achieving your client's goals.

Good ideas don't work for all clients.

If a style, idea or concept isn't chosen by one client; don't be afraid to try it again with another client (if the style, idea or concept still applies).

Only show clients work that you're prepared to stand behind with your name on it.

It's better to ask for more time than present work that is of low quality or doesn't meet the requirements.

Knowing when to compromise for the client is just as important as knowing when not to.

Unfulfilled client expectations lead to a lack of trust and freedom on the next project if there is one.

Be a good listener.

Before you start directing your client you must be able to admit you don't know their product, goals, style or personalities. Figure out who the decision makers are, get to know their personal preferences and then give them exactly what they want but with your own personal style mixed in. It really pays to keep your ego in check and give the client what they want and not just what you want to design for them.

Every client wants fresh new ideas that separate them from their competitors and then ironically want several examples of where those ideas have been done before.

Have pride in your work but not so much pride that you're not willing to compromise or acknowledge the vision of the client paying for your service.

Not every client needs or wants a trend setting design nor can they afford the cost or time it might take to develop it.

Communication is the foundation to any successful client relationship.

Without it ideas fragment, execution suffers, deadlines are missed, and everyone involved will move in different directions towards different goals. Poor communication can taint even award-winning creative projects resulting in the client not returning to you.

Beginning a project on the same page as the client is easy. Staying in sync till the end of a project takes hard work. Being aware of and dedicating yourself towards that goal will make navigating the project much easier.

It's hard to tell a client they're wrong but sometimes it's the only way to gain their trust and respect.

Clients who are vague in describing their goals or visual preferences will more than likely have a difficult time articulating good or bad feedback on your work.

Be prepared to invest more time selling the client on your concepts, designs and decisions if you don't impress them from the project inception.

Always make sure that the client knows you charge extra for reading minds.

Never promise intangible results like awards, press or traffic.

A lot happens from the start to finish of a project, and you don't always have control over all of the variables that make a successful site.

If the client can't articulate their site vision, target audience or company philosophy, it's hard to be effective in actually helping them achieve their goals with a solution tailored specifically to them.

Smaller clients are more likely to take chances.

This can potentially mean some fun, unique and creative opportunities. Unfortunately, the bigger the brand, the more money on the line, the more those projects are scrutinized, micro-managed and often watered down or simplified.

Boring brands do not deserve boring designs. They're often the clients who will let you have fun because they want to be seen as progressive like some of the bigger brands who take chances.

Clients smell insecurity like bears smell fear.

When presenting your work never show doubt in yourself or your ideas. It starts by actually being excited by the work you're presenting. Your passion will shine through like a light at night.

When a client makes a bad feature request, it is NEVER ok to just show them what they asked for in hopes that they'll see what a bad idea it was.

It never works out because they will always choose that solution. If the situation allows, respectfully present alternate solutions that meet the end goal of the original request but don't sacrifice quality.

Become the client.

Mentally pretend that you are a member of the client's team with a fictitious cubicle in a remote part of their office. Be their co-worker or even friend. Get to know everyone on a personal level so that the work you're doing feels more like team collaboration not a vendor/client relationship. You'll do better work when you're emotionally attached to a project and the people involved.

In kickoff meetings encourage the client to talk not just about the project but about their company goals, inspirations and their business.

All of this information will help give you a broader view of the project aside from what is contained in the project brief. When you have a clearer understanding of what your client is doing you will be better equipped to impact not just the project but also their larger business goals.

Clients pay the bills. Without them, we would not have the creative opportunities we have. Keep your ego in check because it is all about them and what they need or want.

It's important to collaborate with and listen to the client.

The client should help you design by advising you on their target audience and establishing the initial goals like how they will measure the success of the site. Companies lacking this basic information should raise an immediate red flag. They should "hopefully" know their target audience and have a vision for what their site is going to accomplish. If they do not, then that company is more than likely going to fail regardless of what you design for them. The client should help you by advising on who they are targeting, provide the images and assets of their products and give you the initial goals and ideas you need to start a design.

When presenting on a project, you're not just selling your design work but also yourself. The client doesn't have to like you, but it helps when they do.

Use words like "we," "our" and "together" when describing the project in meetings.

This serves many purposes. First, it makes the client feel a part of the processes by verbally including them on your team. Second, even if you're the only person designing for the project it gives the client as sense that a bigger team is behind the process and they're getting what they're paying for.

Wasting 30 minutes a day adds up to a potential loss of money over a year.

30 minutes added up over the days, weeks and months of a year add up to **120 hours**. Multiply that by your hourly rate and that is the money you could potentially be losing if you don't manage your time properly. All of those lost hours could be used to do any number of things. Including another project which would mean another opportunity to earn more money, get better as a designer or work on a once in a lifetime project that defines your career.

The agency lifestyle isn't for everyone.

Employment at a well know agency can lead to great opportunities for recognition by working on cutting edge projects. But that perk can come at the cost of a lot of chaos and stress. Unlike working for a brand where campaigns are often planned a year in advance, agency projects typically move at blazing speeds. Your schedule, deadlines and the projects you work on can change day to day and hour by hour. Expect to work late nights, weekends and even holidays because the needs of that new client are what feeds the agency. This life isn't for everyone so be careful what you wish for if your dream is to work on the cool projects.

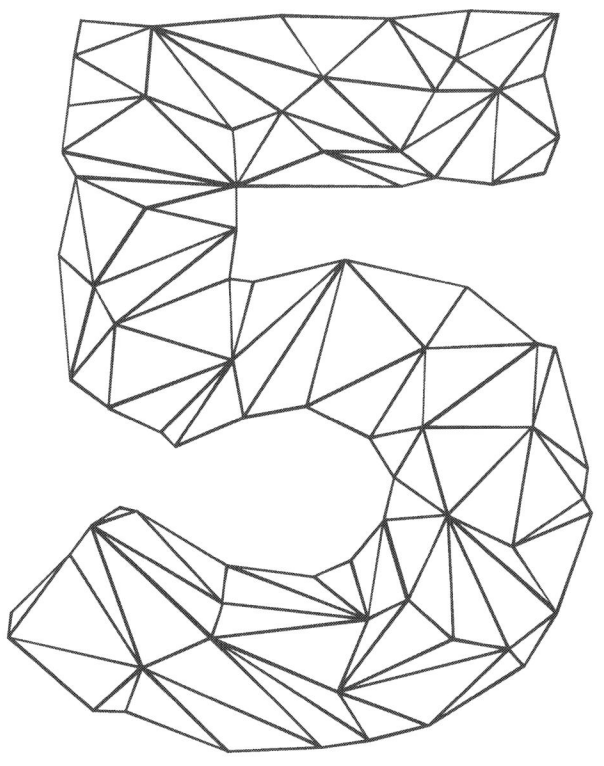

BALANCING LIFE & CAREER

Work hard but play harder

Dream of both the career AND the lifestyle you want. You can have both.

Having a successful career does not mean you must work so hard that you don't have a life. No different than career goals, you must constantly dream of the things you want to accomplish outside of work. Set short-term goals like vacations. Also set big picture long-term life goals, like how you want to buy a house when you start a family. Be relentless in fighting for those goals amongst all of the career noise in your life. There's always someone or something out there trying to distract you from them. Your boss and clients don't want you to grow, change or move on. They want all of your time because that helps them. You are the only person who has your best interests in mind, and it's ok to be selfish for the right things.

Work smarter not longer.

Yes, throwing more hours at a problem is one solution. But such methods are unsustainable and inefficient over time. Work smarter, and you'll have even more time available to work on everything you want both personal and professional.

Have more important things you'd rather be doing outside of work.

Make commitments to do things that you can't get out of. Have family or friends you need to see. Book vacations. Find activities, hobbies, passions and things you'd rather be doing or are already committed to. Meaning, you've already set or planned a time or date to do something else other than work. I've always used this strategy to motivate me to consistently work harder, faster and more intelligently to achieve better work in less time. It has not only made me more effective at what I do but has also given me a world of experiences outside of work I would not have had I only focussed on the project at hand.

Sometimes it's important to learn the skill of saying "NO" by not taking on freelance projects.

Happiness can be a great source of power and creativity. If you're so stressed out and tired from working that you break down, then no amount of extra money is worth it. Pass on the work to a friend for a referral fee and enjoy your free time working on a personal project.

.284

If you don't have a life or interests outside of work, you'll never have anything original to put into your work.

.285

Fight to stay happy and excited about your career.

Boredom or job frustrations are dangerous things. I've seen too many friends consider leaving the industry in their 40s because they're no longer having fun. Fight to maintain that love and passion by working on as many exciting projects as you can. There's nothing better in life than finding something creative that you love to do every day and then getting paid to do it.

Dedication & hard work are requirements for success as a designer. But stepping away from the computer to spend quality time with your friends & family is a requirement for success as a human being. Both are important.

Work should not be the full focus of your energies in life.

Having diversity in your lifestyle has a balancing effect making sure you don't get burnt out allowing you to do better work consistently.

Be careful about letting work control your energy, time or mood.

Leave your baggage and deadlines on your computer. Value every moment you have with those you care about because you can't get that time back and it's not worth losing relationships over work or a project.

Plan vacations first. Worry about projects & deadlines second.

There is never a perfect occasion to take time off. There's always going to be a looming project, deadline or meeting in your life that conflicts. And guess what; those dates & deadlines are always changing so let them fluctuate around your time off. Book trips through the year and use them as motivation to finish your projects more efficiently within shorter times so you can take the time off you need to recharge.

Use all of your vacation days at work.

They are yours to use as part of your employment and if you don't use them you lose them. Don't be pressured by managers or other co-workers who are afraid to take their own days off. In the long run, you'll stay more refreshed throughout the year and potentially have more life experiences to inspire your work.

Don't be the person who is constantly working late.

Leave work by 6 pm at the latest to make sure that you can dedicate at least 3 hours to your family and loved ones during normal evening hours every day. If you need extra time for work, personal exploration, learning a new application or a personal project, establish those hours late at night, over a lunch break, weekends or early in the morning.

Set up a schedule that includes free time.

It's very easy to get caught up with being on the computer working at all hours of the day. It doesn't matter how much money you make on a project or what awards you win, the last thing you want is resentment to build in your friends and family that you're never around to spend quality time.

Play "Mental Tetris" to problem solve in your free time.

Learn to work things out away from a computer by solving problems out spatially in your head. You don't need to be sitting at a computer moving things around on the screen in Photoshop or coding. You can actively problem solve away from the computer in your mind or on a sketch pad.

Family always come first.

If you work so hard chasing career goals like awards, notoriety, promotions or money that you sacrifice the relationships with your friends and family, then you're failing at life. Living is more important than working. Establish boundaries early and then stick to them. Work time is for work. Family time is for family.

If your life outside of work is messed up, your work will suffer too.

Working harder at work won't fix your life problems. So if you are trying to be the best designer, developer, manager, boss you can be it pays to have your own life in order. The analogy I've always used is one from anytime you fly an airplane. The stewardess always gets up there and talks about all of the safety features on the plane. They also then tell you that in case of an emergency an oxygen mask will drop down. They always say make sure to put on your own mask before you try putting on the mask of the person next to you. What this means is. Don't wait for your job to change. Don't wait for your boss to suddenly tell you to stop working less. Don't wait for the perfect relaxed project. Don't wait for the next vacation. Put your oxygen mask on and start changing yourself regardless of the people and events around you.

Fear is a great motivator.

I make a lot of promises and commitments to my wife and family. There is a reason for that. First of all, I'd rather be living than working. But another big reason is that those are commitments I'm afraid to break. I'm more afraid of pissing off my wife or having sad kids than I am about angering a boss or a client. So I use that fear as a motivation not to waste time at work. It helps me to make smart decisions with how I manage my projects so that they don't bleed my time.

Travel to other states and countries.

It is both an inspiring and humbling experience to see much you do not know about the world and how little the world knows or cares about you. Traveling can be especially motivating because if you want to see more of the world, you must have the extra time and money available to do so. Both of which only occur by doing things like: fighting to be visible, working efficiently, getting better projects and being in control of your career.

Learn the words "NO" and "HELP."

Early in my career, I loved the rush of cranking out work over the weekend and sending out that magical 2 am email so that the client knew you'd just spent the weekend or late night working on their project. But just because you can do something doesn't mean you should be expected to do it. Learn to say **NO** to work that doesn't fit within work hours or isn't what you want to do. **Or ask for help.** There's always more time on every project even if we're told there isn't. The hardest part is sending that email asking for more time or being willing to move some deadlines on other projects. But it rarely gets turned down if the need is there. Confining work to normal business hours should be the expectation of everyone.

Establish a "Creative Haven."

It's important to have a separate room at home away from work (and others), that has all of the tools you need for your creative process. Enabling you to escape the noise that can distract you from being productive at night.

Superman never gets any days off.

If you set that precedent as being the person who saves the day on crappy projects or who works at all hours, it's hard to break people from expecting that from you every time. It's great for people to have trust and confidence in you but you don't want to be the person saving the day late at night or on weekends while everyone else is off having fun doing their own personal stuff. Don't answer emails late at night. That suggests that you're doing your work at night and people will expect that. You also don't need to feel obligated to stop everything you're doing to respond to emails the moment you receive them. Especially when you know that it will derail you from tasks you've already started and need to finish.

Play First. Work second.

Sometimes it's hard to stop at the end of the day because you're stuck fixing a bug or want to finish a design or task. This can totally derail you and any plans you might have had to do personal things after work like exercise which is exactly what you need to decompress from work. To prevent this from happening, start off the day doing something for yourself. Get your important personal things out of the way before work like surfing or working out so that you go through the day more relaxed before the chaos hits.

The happier you are with yourself as an individual, the more enjoyable you are to be around.

No one wants to be around someone who is unhappy or grumpy about work all of the time no matter how successful or talented they are.

Problem solve away from the computer on weekends.

I can't tell you how many times I've received an email late Friday afternoon to make changes to something that requires a lot of extra work & thought. Rather than working on it over the weekend (which would affect my personal time), I put the physical aspect of the task off until Monday. But what I will do is think about how to fix the problem all weekend away from the computer. Sometimes we'll be driving somewhere or just hanging out with the kids, and my wife sees the blank expression on my face and will ask. "Everything ok?". My response is always "Yeah...just playing mental Tetris". Which is code for me problem-solving a work related problem. So by Monday I've already thought about and made decisions on how to solve the problem. It always gets done faster than if I'd put in the time over the weekend.

Don't delay vacations.

I used to hate going on vacations. Especially when there was a deadline to worry about because my projects completely consumed me. It got to the point where we never traveled anywhere. Thankfully, I discovered photography and a switch inside of me flipped. Suddenly, the creative opportunity of taking pictures in new places started outweighing work. Over the years, photography has taught me so much about mood, composition, depth and lighting. Using personal photography in your design work also gives you more control over the assets you can bring into projects and gives you instant access to your own personal stock photography. Photography was the catalyst for freeing up my weekends. Any invasion of my weekend plans by work was now like an attack on my family. I now wanted to be more present and enjoy our trips.

They're just websites. We're not curing cancer. No one dies if you miss a deadline.

Of course, try and avoid missing deadlines. But if your constant fear of deadlines means working overtime too often and it's affecting your health or personal life then you need to remember it's ok to ask for more time.

Make the time to teach, mentor or inspire someone. Not only will you make a difference in their life, but the process of teaching will change you as well.

Special Thanks

Special thanks to my wife **Jolene Mielke** for her love, support and forcing me out of my comfort zone all of these years. My daughters **Tristen** & **Taylor** for motivating me to set an example for them by following my own dreams. My parents **Fred & Jane Mielke** for all of their sacrifices to educate me and make me a better person. Douglas Arthur for being my first design mentor/friend and inspiration. Eric Jordan for blazing a pathway for me to follow and encouraging me to make my own. Lukas Ruebbelke for your friendship, constant motivation and willingness to help me stop being such an introvert. Coach Jim Hartigan and Michael Harris who both changed my life at Santa Margarita Catholic High School.

Additional thanks (In Alphabetical Order) to Coach Bob Biggs, Jess Brown, Branislav Cirkovic (Cover & Design Help), Joshua Corliss, Rob Ford, Coach Tony Franks, Marc Hemeon, Matt Hoover, Greg Huntoon, Coach Jamie Larkin, Dan Mall, Jonathan Moore, Matt Norwood, Dan Oliver, Dann Petty, Coach Matt Rink, Elijah Shepard, Coach Dave Uranich, Santa Margarita Catholic High School, The University of California at Davis and all of the others who push, motivate and inspire me on a daily basis.

About the Author

Shane Mielke (aka Pixelranger) is a Freelance Creative Director, Designer, Front-End Developer, Animator, Photographer, Author, Speaker, Coach and Cyberdyne Systems T-1000 Model 101 living in Southern California, USA. For 10 years he was the Creative Director at 2Advanced Studios. He has designed, developed or animated 36 FWA Sites of the Day, 4 FWA Mobile Sites of the day, 2 FWA Sites of the Month, 2 Awwwards and 3 Adobe® Cutting Edge Awards. His work has been featured in over 50 magazines including Advanced Photoshop, Web Designer, Net and Computer Arts Projects. He has also served as a judge for the Adobe® Design Achievement Awards, Flash in the Can Awards, Digital Artist Awards, .net Awards and the prestigious FWA Site of the Year. In 2014 Shane was honored by .Net Magazine as one of the top 50 Designers in the world.

When not reclined in front of the computer and getting minimal hours of sleep, he enjoys spending time with his wife and two daughters, CrossFit, traveling and engaging in the relentless pursuit of photography.

To view his portfolio or find more information visit:
www.shanemielke.com
Twitter: @shanemielke
Instagram: @shanemielke

21166650R00105

Printed in Poland
by Amazon Fulfillment
Poland Sp. z o.o., Wrocław